Flashing
FIRE ENGINES

For Renée, Eric, Cornelia, and Saskia—T.M.

The Publisher thanks London Fire Brigade Headquarters and the
New York City Fire Department Public Information Office for
their kind assistance in the development of this book.

KINGFISHER
a Houghton Mifflin Company imprint
222 Berkeley Street
Boston, Massachusetts 02116
www.houghtonmifflinbooks.com

First published in hardcover in 1998
First published in paperback in 2000
First published in this format in 2005
2 4 6 8 10 9 7 5 3 (POB)
2 4 6 8 10 9 7 5 3 1 (PB)
1TR "UP/0605/SHENS/FR/158MA/C

LIBRARY OF CONGRESS CATALOGING-IN-PUBLICATION DATA
Mitton, Tony.
Flashing fire engines/Tony Mitton, author : Ant Parker, illustrator.
p. cm.
Summary: Rhyming text and illustrations introduce the noisy world of the fire engine.
1. Fire engines—Juvenile literature.   [1. Fire engines.]
I. Parker, Ant. ill. II. Title.
TH9372. M58 1998
628.9'259—dc21   97-51126   CIP AC

ISBN 0-7534-5104-2 (POB)
ISBN 0-7534-5307-X (PB)
ISBN 978-07534-5307-0 (PB)

Printed in Singapore

Flashing
FIRE ENGINES

Tony Mitton
and
Ant Parker

KINGFISHER

BOSTON

Big, bold fire engines, waiting day and night,

ready for a rescue or a blazing fire to fight.

As soon as there's a fire alarm,
the engine starts to roar.

The firefighters jump aboard—
it rumbles out the door.

Watch the engine speeding, on its daring dash.

Hear its siren screaming. See its bright lights flash.

In helmets, fireproof pants and jackets,
boots so big and strong,

the crew is dressed and ready
as the engine zooms along.

When the engine finds the fire,
it quickly pulls up near.

The crew jumps out, unrolls the hose,
and gets out all the gear.

The hose points up its nozzle
and shoots a jet of spray.
It squirts right at the blazing flames
and sizzles them away.

The water tank is empty soon,
so where can more be found?
The engine's pump can pull it up
from pipes below the ground.

The fire is hot and roaring.
It makes a lot of smoke.

The firefighters put on masks,
otherwise they'd choke.

The ladder rises upward. It reaches for the sky.
A fire engine's ladder stretches up so very high!

Sometimes there's a platform, right up at the top.
It waits beside the window. Then into it you hop.

At last the fire's extinguished.
The flames are all put out.

plop!

plop!

Lower the ladder. Roll the hose.
"Hurray!" the fire crew shouts.

Back inside the station,
the crew can take a break.

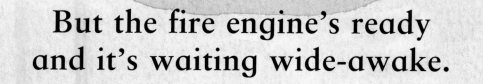

But the fire engine's ready
and it's waiting wide-awake.

Fire Engine parts

helmet

this is a hard hat that protects the firefighter's head

siren

this makes a loud noise to tell people to move out of the way and let the fire engine pass

Fireproof pants and Jackets

these are made from special material that does not burn easily and protects firefighters from the fire

masks and tank

we cannot breathe in smoky air, so firefighters carry clean air in **tanks** on their backs. The air flows into their **masks**

water tank

this is inside the middle of the fire engine and holds water to fight the fire—some fire engines carry foam, too

pump

this sucks water from the tank and pushes it out through huge **hoses**. The pump can also get water from a **hydrant** attached to underground pipes

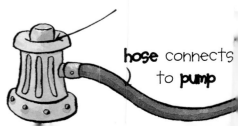

hose connects to **pump**